20th Century Inventions
THE INTERNET

Robert Snedden

RAINTREE
STECK-VAUGHN
PUBLISHERS

A Harcourt Company

Austin · New York
www.steck-vaughn.com

20th Century Inventions

AIRCRAFT

CARS

COMPUTERS

THE INTERNET

LASERS

MEDICAL ADVANCES

NUCLEAR POWER

ROCKETS AND SPACECRAFT

SATELLITES

TELECOMMUNICATIONS

Cover and title page: The Internet allows you to connect with computer users all over the world.

Published by Raintree Steck-Vaughn Publishers, an imprint of Steck-Vaughn Company

Library of Congress Cataloging-in-Publication Data
Snedden, Robert.
The Internet / Robert Snedden.
    p.   cm.—(20th Century Inventions)
    Includes bibliographical references and index.
    Summary: Explains how the Internet has evolved into the massive system that it is today.
    ISBN 0-8172-4815-3
    1. Internet (Computer network)—Juvenile literature.
    [1. Internet (Computer network) 2. Computers.]
    I. Title. II. Series.
    TK5105.875.I57S665 1998
    004.67'8—dc21   97-9068

Printed in Italy. Bound in the United States.
2 3 4 5 6 7 8 9 0 02 01 00 99

Picture acknowledgments
Action-Plus Photographic 31 (bottom); Bryan & Cherry Alexander 23 (both); Paul Bennett 17 (top), 29 (right), 36, 37 (middle); Walt Disney 35 (middle); Image Bank 4 (right)/Andy Zito, 14/Ross M. Horowitz, 15 (top)/C. Alan Wilson, 16/Flip Chalfont, 17 (middle), 18/Michael Coyne, 19 (top)/Steven Dunwell, 32/Jay Freis, 33/Ted Kwai Frskl, 34/Elaine Sulle, 39 (top)/Lou Jones; Image Select 6/Jasmin; Science Photo Library back cover and 3/Tony Craddock, 9/David Parker, 13/Dr Jeremy Burgess, 24/Hank Morgan, 25/David Parker, 29 (top left)/Alex Bartel, 40/Jerry Mason, 41/PH. Plailly/Eurelios, 42 (top)/NASA, 42 (bottom)/Julian Baum, 43 (top)/David Parker; Tony Stone Worldwide 8, 21/Greg Pease, 20 (top)/David Young Wolff, 27/Loren Santow, 28 (left)/Jon Ortner, 37 (bottom)/David Young Wolff, 39/World Perspectives, 43 (bottom)/Peter Cade; TRH Pictures 7 (both); ZEFA front cover and title page. Artwork on pages 8, 11, 12, 26 by Tim Benké, Top Draw (Tableaux). All other pictures Wayland Picture Library.

Find Raintree Steck Vaughn on the Internet at http://www.steck-vaughn.com

CONTENTS

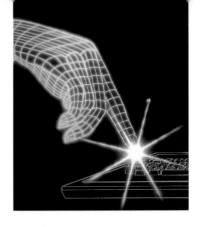

INTRODUCTION

Where on Earth is the Internet?

We often hear or read about people using the Internet, or the "Net," as it is often called. You may even have used it yourself, perhaps at home or at school. If you have, you know it has something to do with computers, because you have used your personal computer (PC) to gain access to the Internet. But what exactly is it you are logging on to?

Computers can be linked by networks (see page 10), allowing them to share information. The Internet is a supernetwork of networks, with millions of computers, scattered over the world, joined together. There is no single master computer "running the Internet." No one is in charge of this worldwide network.

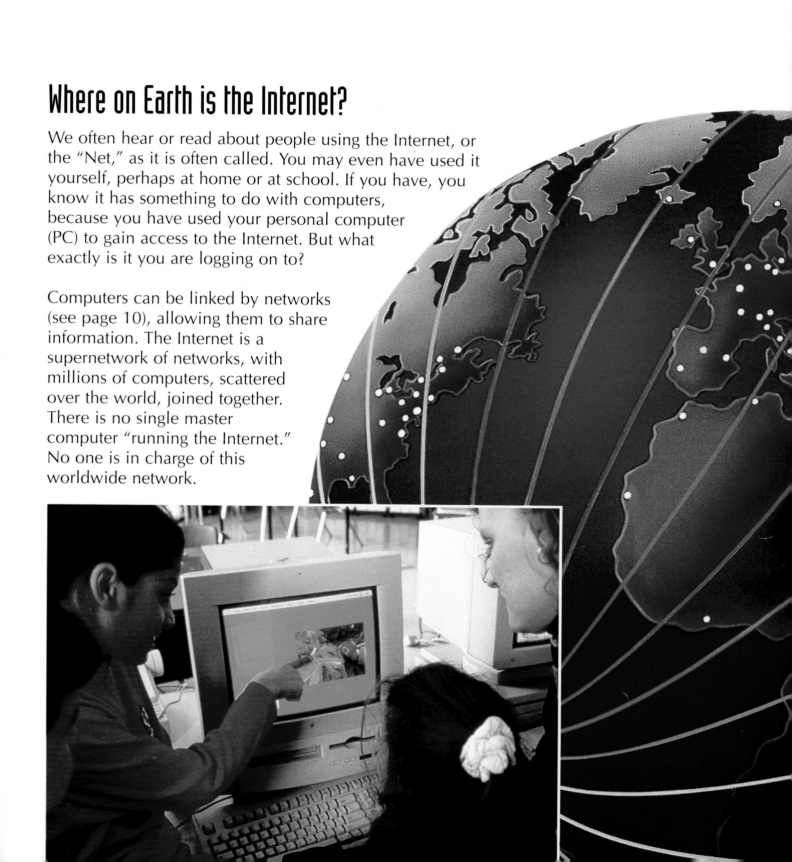

The Internet can be described as a constant flow of information from place to place and person to person. Whenever you access the Internet, you have the potential of being linked to tens of millions of other computer users. Some of them will have things of interest to share with you and will want to hear what you have to say.

Most of all the Internet is about people. It is a worldwide, twenty-four-hour-a-day meeting place where anyone can join in. It does not matter who you are, what you look like, what you wear, or where you are. Sometimes people are argumentative or rude. But most of the time you find people who are friendly and helpful on the Internet. Be polite and considerate, and others will treat you in the same way.

Above and opposite **The Internet allows you to connect with computer users on the other side of the world. It could also change the face of education, allowing students to "log on" to school without leaving home.**

Cyberspace

You may well have heard of the term "cyberspace." It was invented by the novelist William Gibson in his book, *Neuromancer,* in the early 1980s. It means the electronic world of networked computers where information is held and retrieved (recovered or got back) and conversations take place across thousands of miles (kilometers). It is not the same as the Internet, but maybe it is where the Net is.

IN THE BEGINNING . . .

In the early 1960s, the United States and the Soviet Union—the world's most powerful countries, or superpowers—were in the middle of what was known as the Cold War. Both countries spent a great deal of time and money trying to outdo each other in terms of the weapons they produced, and in trying to ensure that an attack could be successfully defended. One of the problems the United States looked at was how to keep communications open after a nuclear strike by the Soviet Union.

It was impossible to design a communications network that had parts that were so well-protected that they could withstand the power of a nuclear explosion. It was also impossible to defend a command center, which would be one of the first things targeted by enemy missiles. So what was the solution?

ARPANET

The RAND Corporation, a think-tank, or organization that researches problems, came up with a daring answer. There would be no central command, and the network would be designed to keep operating even if some of its parts, or nodes, were destroyed. Every node would be equal to every other node. Each one would be able to send and receive messages to and from every other node, so there was no single route through the network. Messages would be divided into packets and sent through the network.

A military parade in the former Soviet Union. Like so many other inventions, the Internet grew from the needs of the military. The U.S. Department of Defense needed to defend its communications network from a Russian nuclear attack.

Each packet would take a different route and meet again at the intended address. It would not matter if some parts of the network were missing. Any node that received a packet would be able to send it on in the direction of its destination by the routes that remained intact even if it meant going by the longest route.

The first test network, based on these ideas, was set up by the National Physical Laboratory in Great Britain in 1968. Shortly afterward, the Advanced Research Projects Agency (ARPA), part of the U.S. Department of Defense, began work on a more complex network, using the fastest available computers at the time as nodes. By December 1969, four computers were linked by high-speed lines to form the ARPANET.

If the Americans were to respond effectively to an attack by the Russians, it was essential that contact could be maintained with the missile bases. Here, officers at a command post monitor the firing of a Titan II missile.

Mailing lists

A way of sending an identical message by electronic mail, or e-mail, to a large number of subscribers on the ARPANET was soon discovered. This meant that people with a shared interest could exchange information and opinions with others in the group. This was called a mailing list. One of the first and most popular lists was concerned with science fiction. Today there are hundreds of different mailing lists. You will find a few examples on page 45.

HERE COMES THE INTERNET

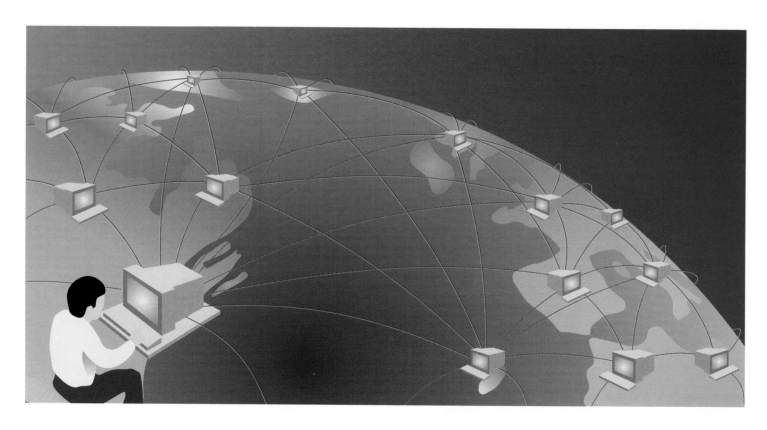

A network of computers in which there are many routes information can follow from computer to computer. If one computer link fails, the data can be rerouted.

ARPANET allowed scientists and researchers to share computer facilities over long distances. By 1971 ARPANET had fifteen nodes, and by 1972 it had thirty-seven. However, it was not being used entirely for the purpose its makers intended.

Most of the messages being sent on the ARPANET were personal ones. People had their own addresses for e-mail and were making use of this to exchange ideas and often just to have a "chat." In fact, this was a far more popular use than long-distance computing. The military thought that this was not good for security, so they formed their own network, called MILNET, in the early 1980s.

In the beginning, ARPANET used something called the Network Control Protocol to control the transfer of information between its computers. Eventually this was replaced by the more sophisticated TCP/IP. Transmission Control Protocol (TCP) converts messages into packets to be sent, and then puts them back together into messages when they reach their destination.

Internet Protocol (IP) takes care of addressing the packets and ensures that each one can be sent across different nodes in the network, or even between networks. TCP/IP was made available to anyone who wanted to use it. By 1977 other fast-growing networks were linked to ARPANET, using TCP/IP. ARPANET, the original network, became a less important part of the network of networks that was coming into existence. By 1990 it disappeared altogether.

These supercomputers at the University of Illinois are part of the National Science Foundation Network (NSFNET). Scientists can use modems to link into the network from their workstations, giving them access to great computing power.

The Internet arrives

In 1986 the U.S. National Science Foundation set up NSFNET connecting top-of-the-line supercomputers with high-speed links, which allowed information, or data, to be transferred between supercomputers at fast rates. It also created regional networks to link schools and universities in an area and then joined these regional networks to the NSFNET.

By the mid–1980s, more than 50,000 computer nodes were linked into what was becoming known as the Internet. Computers in countries as far apart as New Zealand, India, and Brazil joined. In the early 1990s, commercial businesses were allowed on to the Internet for the first time. Ordinary people, without access to universities or big research institutions, could set up their own Internet accounts through the growing number of service providers (see page 17) that were being established. Today there are more than a million nodes scattered around the world, linking tens of millions of people, each one with a unique e-mail address.

NETWORKS

What exactly is a network? In the world of computers, a network simply means two or more computers linked in some way. The purpose of this network is to allow people in different places to communicate with one another and to share data and resources. For example, a school or a business might have a big central computer, called a server, that stores various programs and files. If someone on the network, using another computer, wants to use one of the files on the server, his or her computer would retrieve that file from the server, using a program called a client program.

Having important files in a central location allows many different users to have easy access to them. The Internet works in the same way. A Web browser, such as Netscape Navigator®, is one example of a client program used on the Internet. Netscape Navigator® is run from a computer to retrieve information from another computer acting as the server. On the Internet you have access to millions of servers all over the world.

Computers are a vital part of modern businesses. In a large organization, most of the computer users will be able to communicate with one another and share information across a network.

A Local Area Network (LAN) connects all the computers on it to one another directly, usually by a cable. If your school has several computers, they may be connected by a LAN. Any computer on a network is called a host or a node. To get information on the network, you must connect your computer in some way to one of the host computers.

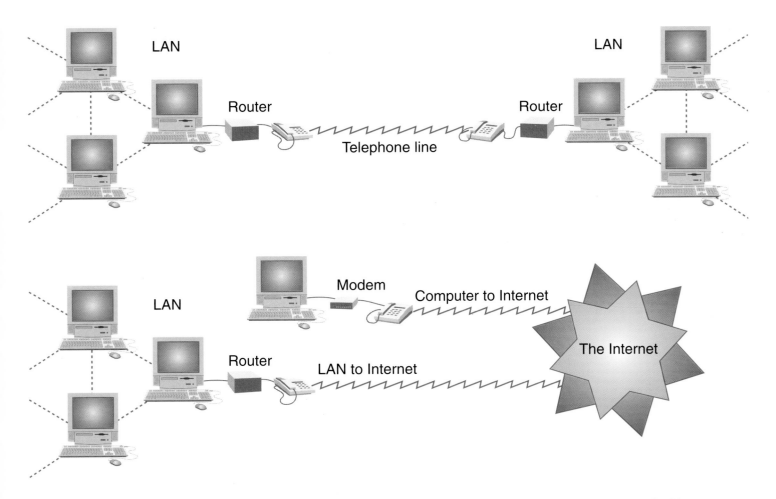

The formation of WANs

In a university or a big business, where there are lots of computers in different departments, the connections get more complex. There may be several LANs connecting each department's computers. Each LAN is connected to a high-speed link called a backbone, usually by a telephone line. Together the LANs plus the backbone form a Wide Area Network (WAN). The backbone can also provide a link to computers in other locations.

Computers called routers are used to link one network to another and keep the data traffic flowing smoothly. They connect LANs to WANs and WANs to bigger WANs. If you have two or more networks linked together, you have an internet, and the biggest internet of all is, of course, the Internet.

Top **Two LANs linked by a telephone line to form a WAN.** Bottom **Networks or individual computers can be linked into the biggest WAN of all, the Internet.**

LET'S GET CONNECTED

What do you need to get connected to the Internet? First, you need some hardware—the computers themselves—either at school or at home.

Any computer capable of running the programs needed for access to the Internet will do—it might be a Macintosh compatible or an IBM compatible, for example. Ask a parent or family friend to find out if your computer can run the programs you need.

Modems

The hardware you need for an internet connection: a computer, a modem, and a telephone line.

Next, you need a modem (short for MOdulator-DEModulator). A modem allows computers to communicate with each other through the telephone system. It dials the telephone number you are using to connect you to the Internet.

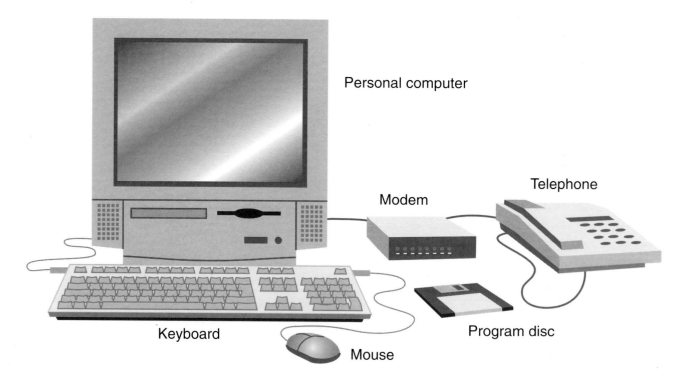

Personal computer

Modem

Telephone

Keyboard

Mouse

Program disc

The Internet makes use of the same communications network of telephone lines and satellite links that you would use for making an ordinary telephone call.

Then it takes the data you want to send from your computer and puts it into a form that can be sent through the telephone line (called modulation). Then when data comes back through the line to you, the modem puts it back into a form your computer will understand (called demodulation).

The modem uses the same telephone line you would use to make an ordinary telephone call. Your computer may come with a modem already fitted inside it, or the modem can be plugged into the back of your computer. Your computer needs software to talk to the modem. This usually comes on a disc packaged with the modem.

Bandwidth

In your Internet travels you might come across the term "bandwidth." It is used to describe the amount of data that can pass through a connection at any one time. The more people trying to get information from a particular source on the Internet, the more demands there are on the bandwidth. High demand slows things down. So if you are accessing a popular site, be prepared for a slow download even if you have a fast modem.

Microwave relay stations are an important part of the communications network. For example, they are used to send signals from a telephone exchange, across the landscape, to the nearest satellite ground station.

The faster the modem, the better. Modem speed is measured in bits per second (bps). It takes eight bits to send or receive a single letter or number. The fastest available modems at the moment run at 33,600 bps. This means you could transmit all of this section in about a quarter of a second. Slower modems will connect you, but you may have to wait a while for files to appear on your screen since the data will take a long time to move from one place to another.

Software

You also need to have the right software. A variety of programs are available, which are designed to perform different tasks on different machines. There are programs for sending and receiving e-mail. There are programs that allow you to search databases for files you can copy, or download, onto your computer, using File Transfer Protocol (FTP), the standard way of moving a file from one computer to another on the Internet.

At the ground station, a large dish antenna (left) sends the signals up to a satellite orbiting the earth (above). The signals are aimed back to a receiving ground station that sends them on to a telephone exchange. The system allows communications to be passed from one country to another in a fraction of a second.

There are programs called browsers that give you access to the World Wide Web.

Finally it is unlikely that you will have a direct link to the Internet, like universities, so you will need to find a service provider (see page 17).

BBS, ONLINE SERVICES, AND SERVICE PROVIDERS

There are three main ways for ordinary users to access the online world: bulletin boards, online services, and service providers.

Bulletin boards

Bulletin board systems, or services (BBSs), are computer systems that allow subscribers to download files and exchange messages with other people on the BBS. A BBS can be quite small, and many are aimed at people living in a certain area or who have a shared interest. It is not the same as being on the Internet, but some BBSs do allow limited access to the Internet, such as being able to send and receive e-mail.

Online services

In some ways, online services are like very big bulletin boards. Increasingly they are providing full access to the Internet, but they are not considered part of the Internet itself. An online service is often a good place to find information because it is well organized with plenty of help available if you need it. One of the best-known online services is CompuServe®. It gives you access to the latest news, weather reports, train schedules, online encyclopedias, and discussion groups, called forums, where you can get files and exchange messages on a wide range of topics. CompuServe® provides full Internet access to members as well. Its biggest rival is America Online® (AOL), which expanded into Europe in 1996. The Microsoft Network® (MSN) is also set to be a major online service.

Above and opposite **By going online you can find out when the trains are running, complete a homework assignment, or find a fun place to visit.**

Service providers

For the average person, the service provider is their gateway to the Internet. The service provider itself has a direct, twenty-four-hour-a-day connection to the Internet, and in exchange for a fee it allows subscribers to have access to that connection through their modems.

A good service provider supplies you with all the programs you need to access the Internet. It provides an e-mail program and a program to connect your computer to the Internet, such as MacTCP for Macintosh computers and Trumpet Winsock for IBM computers.

A service provider can be cheaper than an online service since many give unlimited access to the Internet for a monthly fee. An online service often charges you for every hour that you go over a certain amount of time. In choosing a service provider, one very important consideration is whether or not you can dial it by using a local telephone number to keep costs down. A big service provider offers a number of points of presence, or PoPs—a group of telephone numbers that you can use to dial into the service.

It can sometimes be fairly complicated setting up the connection to a provider—a good provider has a telephone helpline to give you all the help and advice you need.

IN TOUCH WITH THE WORLD

E-mail

Imagine being able to send a letter to someone anywhere in the world, which included sights and sounds as well as written words, and not even having to put a stamp on it. With e-mail you can do just that. E-mail allows you to send messages quickly and easily to other people, using computers rather than the postal service. To the Internet user, the ordinary postal service is known as "snail mail" because it is so much slower than e-mail, which can deliver its message to the other side of the world in seconds.

In some ways e-mail is like a cross between a letter and a telephone call. You type a note or a letter on your screen, and then you send it through the telephone line to another person for as little as it costs you to call your service provider. Whether your message is going to Calgary in Canada, or to Copenhagen in Denmark, it will cost the same. You can even attach a file from your computer, whether it be a sound, an image, or text, to your e-mail message.

Here I am!

E-mail addresses are made up of two distinct parts, separated by the "@" sign. The first part of the address identifies the specific user. Many people use their names, their initials, their nickname, or, in the case of a business address, their title. After the @ sign comes the host address or node name, which is the actual place where the user's electronic mailbox is situated. Here is an example. To send e-mail to the people who run Kid's Web (see page 36) you would use the address feedback@kidscom.com. "Feedback" is the name used for the people who take questions and comments. "Kidscom" is the name of the company providing the server.

When a new user joins the Internet for the first time, he or she will acquire a unique e-mail address that allows the user to send and receive messages. Just as you need to put the correct address on an envelope to make sure it gets to the right place, you must also put the correct e-mail address on your electronic correspondence. Computers are not as understanding as postal workers, who can sometimes figure out where an incorrectly addressed letter is meant to go. If you make a slight mistake with your address, the nodes on the Internet cannot guess what you meant to put. Your message will simply be bounced back to you.

Above and opposite **Using e-mail, you can send messages quickly and cheaply to people all over the world.**

Where are you?

How do you find out what someone's e-mail address is? The easiest and best way is simply to ask them. Since there is no one in charge of the whole Internet and because it is expanding so rapidly, there is no complete record of everyone who is connected.

USING E-MAIL PROGRAMS

When someone sends you a message by e-mail, it is stored on the computer at your service provider. If your school has its own connection to the Internet, it is stored on the main server. Once you have logged on to the Net, you can launch your e-mail program. Eudora® is one of the most popular and easy-to-use programs and is available for both Macintosh and IBM compatibles. There is a version that you can download free of charge from the Internet. Many programs will automatically search for new messages when they are first launched.

E-mail has obvious advantages for schools and businesses that want to keep track of their messages. For example, it allows you to quote all or part of the message you are replying to, without having to retype it. If you are answering questions, this feature is great because you can keep the questions in your reply. This saves the other person having to refer to the original document when he or she gets your reply.

E-mail also allows you to forward a message to someone else. If someone sends you information that you feel would be of interest to another person, you can send on a copy of the message with your own ideas and comments attached.

E-mail is invaluable for large organizations that might have offices scattered all over the world. For example, someone in the London office might send a query or a new idea to someone else in New York. The person in New York might realize that this is something that another person in Sydney, Australia, has been working on, and passes on the message almost instantly.

Above and opposite **E-mail is a fun way of sharing information about the activities you do at school, such as going on a field trip or making unusual sounds in a music lesson, with children in different parts of the world.**

Attaching files

If you want to send a graphics file (one containing a picture), a sound file, a document, or a video clip with your e-mail, you can do that, too. Most e-mail readers have menu items that allow you to attach a file using an instruction, or command, called "attach file" or something similar. To do this the e-mail program uses MultiPurpose Internet Mail Extensions (MIME) to attach the file and process it into the chunks of the right size for sending by e-mail.

Schools and businesses can use this facility to exchange information, such as project findings and ideas for new products, complete with sounds and pictures, to make everything clear. Unlike a mailed letter, receivers can add it directly into their own files and change it, if they wish, to suit their own needs, because this information goes directly to the receiver's computer.

What's in a name?

Because e-mail only exists electronically, you cannot take a pen and sign your letter in the normal way. However, e-mail programs do allow you to attach a "signature" to the end of all your correspondence. This might be in the form of your "snail mail" address, a joke, a favorite quotation, or something else that tells the receiver something about you. Some people even make cartoons, using just letters and symbols. Whatever you do, keep it simple. Remember that people at the other end are using their time to download your signature.

SIMPLY SAY IT

If the Internet has any lasting effect on our lives, it may well be through the use of e-mail. As we have seen, there are many advantages that e-mail has over snail mail in terms of speed and usefulness. It also has a big advantage over a message taken over the telephone—you cannot print out a telephone call. More people probably join the Internet to get access to e-mail than for any other reason.

Many people use abbreviations for certain phrases. Here are a few of them:

BTW	**by the way**
FAQ	**frequently asked questions**
FYI	**for your information**
<G>	**grin**
IMHO	**in my humble opinion**
LOL	**laughing out loud**
ROTFL	**rolling on the floor laughing**
TTYL	**talk to you later**

Then there are "smileys," or emoticons, which are used to try and give a little bit of expression to printed messages. These are just for fun. If you do not see the "faces," try turning the book sideways.

:-)	**happy**
:-(	**sad**
:-o	**shocked**
:-P	**sticking your tongue out**
:-&	**tongue-tied**
;-)	**winking**

E-mail is easy to use, and it saves time and money. The differences in time throughout the world do not matter when sending e-mail. It is a twenty-four-hour service that allows you to send information at any time of the day or night. If you want to know what it is like to live in the Arctic, send a message to a school in Alaska and find out. If a company wants to know how much it costs to print a book in the Far East, it can e-mail some printers in Singapore or Hong Kong. The message will be there the next time someone at the other end switches on the computer and logs on. No one has to be there to answer the telephone. It does not matter if they are in bed when you send the message or if you are watching a movie at the theater when they send a reply.

Netiquette

If you want to make friends on the Internet, remember to have good manners. One of the most important rules to follow is, DON'T TYPE ALL OF YOUR MESSAGES IN CAPITAL LETTERS. It is the Internet equivalent of shouting into the telephone. Be careful how you say things. Because it is so fast and easy to send e-mail messages, people often do not bother to check what they have written before pressing the "send" button. Compose your e-mail with the same care and attention you would use for other forms of communication. Reply to your messages promptly. If someone has taken the trouble to write to you, take the time to write back. It is only polite.

Do you want to know what it is like to live in the Arctic? Send e-mail to a school there and find out. Electronic communications help the remotest communities stay in touch with the world.

WEAVING THE WEB

One of the most exciting developments on the Internet is the World Wide Web (WWW or the "Web"). The Web is one of the best ways of exploring the Internet because it gives you not only text, but also pictures and sounds. The Web connects thousands of computers and millions of files all over the world. It is made up of a vast collection of sites, which could be businesses, universities, government organizations, or individuals renting space from their Internet service provider.

In the early 1980s, more and more information was becoming available to the growing number of scientists who had access to the infant Internet. However, finding the information they wanted was not always an easy task. If they wanted to download a piece of information, they needed to know which computer it was stored on, where the computer was, how to contact it, which program they had to run to get the information, and how to use that program. Finding their way around on the young Internet could be a difficult process. A way had to be found to allow scientists across the world fast access to work being done elsewhere, so that they could keep up-to-date with developments and make their own contributions to the new discoveries.

Tim Berners-Lee, the British computer scientist who revolutionized the Internet. By creating the World Wide Web, he created a way of sharing information across the Internet that was much easier to use than anything that had come before.

The Web spinner

Tim Berners-Lee, a British computer scientist working for the European High Energy Particle Physics Laboratory (CERN) in Switzerland wanted to create a way for people to get at the information on computer networks without having to worry about software and complicated commands. In 1989 he put forward a project that he called the World Wide Web. It was designed to allow people to work together by combining their knowledge in a way that made it easy to follow links from one topic to another. The World Wide Web program first appeared at CERN in December 1990, and by the summer of the following year it was available on the Internet.

The Web made accessing the Internet easy. Berners-Lee gave the computers a language to talk to each other that allowed computer users simply to point and click at things on their screens. People did not need to know how to navigate their way through the Internet's complex connections to find the information they wanted—the Web would do it for them. According to Berners-Lee, the Internet is "a collection of cables ...and machines," while the Web is "a pure information space," in other words, an "area" filled with information. The thing that allowed people to follow a path through this information space was hypertext (explained on the next page).

A computer scientist at CERN, the Particle Physics Laboratory in Switzerland where the World Wide Web was first created. He is updating pages of information that will be studied by scientists in many countries. Web pages can be located at computers all over the world, not just at CERN.

HYPERTEXT AND BROWSERS

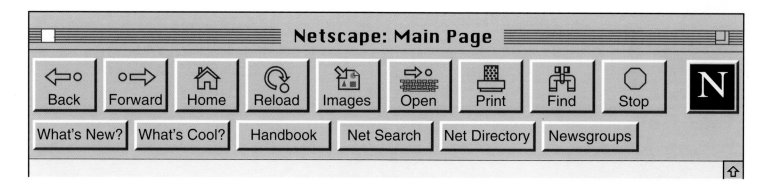

Internet browsers allow you to navigate through the great sea of information that is available on the Internet and the World Wide Web in particular.

Hypertext revolutionized the Internet. When you look at a Web document on your screen, some words appear in bold type, like this: **bold-faced words represent hypertext links**. Click on a bold word or phrase, and your computer downloads information from another computer on the Web and displays it to you. You do not have to worry about where the other computer might be: The Web will take you there.

The Web makes use of Hypertext Markup Language (HTML), the computer code that is used to write Web pages. HTML can present text, images, sound files, and video, all within a single document, and also can create links between one page and another.

Browsing the Web

Each site contains a number of Web pages with hypertext links to other files and pages on that site, or perhaps on Web sites halfway around the world. Using your computer's mouse, you simply point and click on the selected word or graphic, and the Web takes you through cyberspace to the new location.

In order to use the Web, you will need a browser. This is a program that allows you to see the information stored on the Web. There are several browsers, probably one of the best of which is Netscape Navigator®. Microsoft's Internet Explorer® is also highly regarded.

To get connected to a Web site, you must type in the correct address.

What's that address?

Every Web site has an address called a Uniform Resource Locator (URL). The URL may be quite long and is broken down into the type of site://name of computer/file directory/file name/. Here's an example: The Electronic Zoo: http://netvet.wustl.edu/e-zoo/e-zoo.htm.

The first portion of the URL, "http" (Hypertext Transfer Protocol), shows that it is a site that contains hypertext (most Web addresses begin with "http" and if you use Netscape Navigator®, you do not have to type that part in every time); "netvet.wustl.edu" is the name of the computer you will connect to; "edu" tells you it is at an educational establishment, usually a university; "e-zoo" is the file directory on the computer that you will open.

CLICKING AROUND THE WORLD

Exploring the Web is a really fun and easy way to spend some time. Sometimes you do not know where you are going to end up from one click to the next. You may begin by logging on to a computer in the United States, but the next click could take you to Canada, Great Britain, Australia, Denmark, or who knows where?

Your journey begins at your "home page," which is the first page your browser loads when you start it up. It is possible to make this any page you want. You might choose a search engine (see page 30) as your start-up page.

Whatever or wherever your starting point might be, the Internet can take you around the world on your search for fun and information. The cities shown are New York City (below), London, England (right), and Perth, Australia (far right).

There is no risk of getting lost in the Web. Your browser keeps track of where you have been, keeping a list of all the sites you have visited in each session. This allows you to retrace your steps if you end up going down one of the Internet's blind alleys.

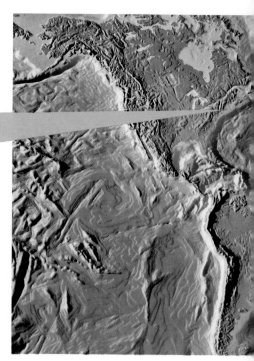

Keeping addresses

Everytime you find a site that you like and want to come back to, you can keep a record of it using your browser's "bookmark," "hotlist," or "favorites" option, depending on the browser you are using. This lets you keep a list of the addresses of your favorite sites for easy access. This way you do not have to type the address each time you want to go back there.

You can also save time if you turn off the graphics display in your browser. Doing this means that only text is downloaded to your computer, which is much faster. Your browser shows you the "hole" where the graphics would be. If you think something might be worth looking at, you need only click on the graphics icon to download the image. Use the "save" option in your browser to keep a copy of an interesting file on your computer. It helps to keep telephone charges down if you read a file offline rather than doing it while you are connected.

SEARCHING AND RETRIEVING

Here are some starting points for your Internet travels. The results of a search engine inquiry are a list of hypertext links to the sites that fit the topic you asked for. Just click on the one that looks most promising and away you go.

Lycos

Lycos, at http://www.lycos.com, is one of the biggest search engines. It was developed in 1994 by Michael Mauldin at Carnegie Mellon University in Pittsburgh, Pennsylvania. It covers more than 90 percent of the Web.

Search engines are the key to unlocking the Internet's treasures. Alta Vista uncovered over 7,000 sites with information on solar power.

Alta Vista

Alta Vista, at http://altavista.digital.com, is operated by the Digital Equipment Corporation. It is perhaps the largest Web index, accessing over 30 million Web pages and handling over 23 million queries every day.

Yahooligans!

Yahooligans!, at http://www.yahooligans.com, was developed by the same people who produce Yahoo! (www.yahoo.com), one of the best organized and laid out indexes for the Web. Yahooligans! was produced with children in mind and has a number of fun links.

File transfer protocol (FTP)

FTP connects one computer to another to allow the transfer of files between them. Popular FTP programs are Fetch® (for the Macintosh computers) and CuteFTP® (for IBM computers). The file libraries available on the Internet include many examples of programs for getting the best out of the Internet.

You can even download whole books and games through FTP. Most FTP sites allow members of the public to log on as "anonymous," which is why you may come across the term "anonymous FTP." If the site asks you for a password, either the word "guest" or your e-mail address will probably work.

Remember that the site is actually on a working computer, perhaps at a university, that is doing other jobs as well. Because of this, the people running the site limit the number of people from outside who can log on at any one time. So try again later if you do not get on the first time.

There are several programs available that search the Internet in various ways. Archie helps you to find FTP files, although its searches can be slow. Gopher lets you find all types of information, such as text and sound files, using lists of options, or menus.

However, the best way to find your way around is to get on the Web. So if you do not already have one on your computer, make a search for Netscape Navigator®, or another browser, a priority. Once you have it you can make use of FTP and Gopher or just surf the Internet all with one program.

Search engines can also help you to keep up-to-date with news and sporting events. Many, such as Infoseek (www.infoseek.com), have built-in news gathering facilities.

THE INTERNET AT WORK

E-mail and the Internet, along with other telecommunications inventions, allow many people to work from home at times that suit them.

The Internet has the potential to transform the way people do business with one another, particularly when that business involves processing information. A lot of office work, for instance, can be done at a distance. That is what is meant by "teleworking" or "telecommuting." There is a lot of talk about changing patterns of work in the electronic world as people create offices anywhere they plug in a computer and a modem. It makes no difference whether you connect to the company server from the next room or the next country. Using a laptop computer and a mobile telephone, you could even be on a ship traveling between countries.

Intranets

An intranet is like a miniature Internet—a private section of cyberspace that operates within an organization. Using Internet software and technology, in particular Web browsers, an intranet gives an organization the ability to communicate in new ways with its employees. It allows departments within the company to share information with one another, speeding project development and allowing people to make positive contributions.

Intranets, like miniature Internets, allow the employees of a large company to share information quickly and easily.

One, or even all, of the organization's computers can act as web servers, storing web pages and programs that allow employees to access company databases. Employee handbooks and manuals can be published on the company intranet where all the information can be found simply by typing in a key word. The manuals can be kept up-to-date without the expense of having to send them to the printer every time something changes.

The company telephone directory can become far more than just a list of numbers. Employees can look up someone by name, department, or geographical location, and send an e-mail message to them at the click of a button. Contracts and other customer-related information can be stored in searchable databases, allowing employees to find information and answer customer questions much quicker than before.

In fact any information relevant to the company, from product specifications, sales figures, and job vacancies within the organization, to profiles of rival organizations and their products, can be placed in searchable databases. For organizations with offices and factories in several countries, the benefit of having researchers in different parts of the world contributing directly to one another's work is enormous. For example, a technician with a problem can search the company web to see if anyone else has had similar difficulties and find out how he or she solved it.

THE INTERNET AT HOME

Many companies already make their goods and services available online, and the number is increasing as time goes by. It is now possible to check train and plane schedules and make reservations online. You can also order flowers, books, food, and clothes, as well as many other items.

If you know what you want, then this is a convenient way to order goods without having to visit a store, although some people will always prefer to see and touch something in "real life" before buying it. Of course, no one is going to repair your refrigerator over the Internet, and until *Star Trek*-like transporters are invented someone still has to deliver your purchase to your home.

For those who live in remote places, the ability to conduct business over the Internet provides many benefits. Using the Internet, they can place an order with a company and pay for the goods, using a credit card. The company can take the order without having to employ people to take the call.

The last thing credit card users want is for someone else to discover their number when they pay for an order on the Internet. Security filters on browsers such as Netscape Navigator® allow people to send personal details to retailers online without fear of interception by anyone else.

Search agents are being developed that will scan all the available prices of a particular product and let you know where you can find the best price. Bargain Finder Agent (http://bf2.cstar.ac.com/bf/), for example, checks prices of CDs. Understandably such search agents are not popular with some retailers who refuse to let their prices be broadcast in this way.

Above and opposite **Besides providing a wealth of information, the Internet gives you access to many other services, such as travel agents and entertainment guides, from the comfort of your home.**

What's news?

You can also read newspapers, or at least electronic versions of them, online. *The Gate* (www.sfgate.com) is published by the *San Francisco Chronicle and Examiner*. *The Hindu* (www. webpage.com/hindu/) is the online version of one of India's most popular newspapers, and *The Electronic Telegraph* (http://www.telegraph. co.uk) is a highly regarded, award-winning version of London's *Daily Telegraph* newspaper.

Online news lets you do things you cannot do with ordinary newspapers, such as find background information on the stories that interest you. Try searching for newspapers from around the world and finding out how important events are reported in different countries.

What's happening?

Many states have regional websites to allow residents to find out what is happening in their neighborhoods. New Jersey Online (www.nj.com) gives details on everything from major concerts to movies at your local theater. And, if you want to read a review of a movie before you go, you might try Excite Movie Reviews at http://www.excite.com/reviews/movies.

INFORMATION AND EDUCATION

Penfriends online

Imagine you are doing a project about a foreign country. It would be very helpful if you could ask someone who lives there to tell you about it. You can, using e-mail. Just contact the mailing list pen-pals-request@mainstream.com, with the message "subscribe pen-pals." Or try Kidlink (http://www.kidlink.org), which offers a variety of forums for children ages ten to fifteen to exchange ideas and information with one another. As well as getting the information you are looking for, you might make a new friend.

Help with homework

If you need some help with your homework, then the Internet might just be the place to look. Yahooligans! (see page 30) is a good place to start, as is Kids' Web: A World Wide Digital Library for Schoolkids (www.kidsweb.org), which has some excellent links to sites of interest to children and to adults as well. The Internet Public Library (http://www.ipl.org) is packed with information and exhibitions and is well worth a look.

Visit a museum

Museums are good places to find information, and there are now several that you can visit through the Internet. The Exploratorium in San Francisco, California (http://www.exploratorium.edu), is an excellent introduction to the world of science and technology. The Natural History Museum in London (http://www.nhm.ac.uk) provides details about the latest exhibits and events at the museum, as well as a selection of images to download and links to other topics of interest. The WebMuseum in Paris, France, has a wonderful site (http://watt.emf.net/louvre) that will take you on a tour of some of the art treasures held there and provide you with detailed background information on the artists and their work.

Planning a vacation abroad? The Internet can provide you with a huge range of information about the best places to visit, such as Uluru (Ayers Rock) in Australia (right), the Stanley Park totems in Vancouver, Canada (opposite top), or simply a beach where it is warm all year long.

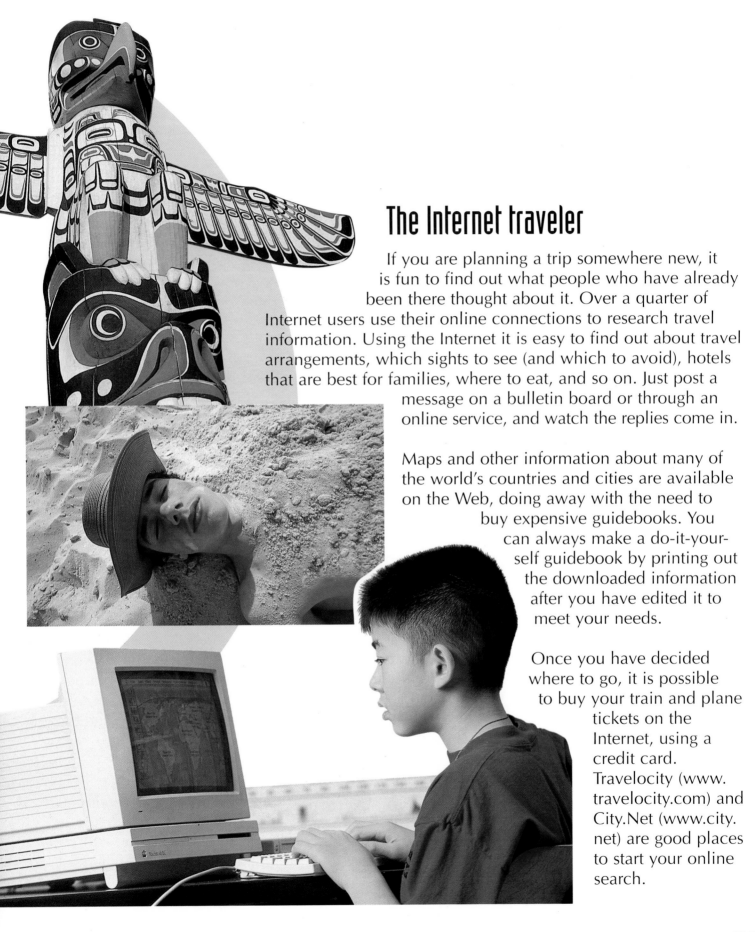

The Internet traveler

If you are planning a trip somewhere new, it is fun to find out what people who have already been there thought about it. Over a quarter of Internet users use their online connections to research travel information. Using the Internet it is easy to find out about travel arrangements, which sights to see (and which to avoid), hotels that are best for families, where to eat, and so on. Just post a message on a bulletin board or through an online service, and watch the replies come in.

Maps and other information about many of the world's countries and cities are available on the Web, doing away with the need to buy expensive guidebooks. You can always make a do-it-yourself guidebook by printing out the downloaded information after you have edited it to meet your needs.

Once you have decided where to go, it is possible to buy your train and plane tickets on the Internet, using a credit card. Travelocity (www. travelocity.com) and City.Net (www.city. net) are good places to start your online search.

SCHOOLS ON THE INTERNET

Many of the pictures taken by the Hubble Space Telescope are available on the Internet. For a really good selection, try http://www.stsci.edu/pubinfo/Pictures.html.

School magazines

Midlink Magazine is an electronic magazine aimed at children ages ten to fifteen. Visitors to the site are invited "to enjoy art and writing that will link middle school kids all over the world." Its URL is http://longwood.cs.ucf.edu/~MidLink.

Kidpub gives you the chance to see your work on the Internet. It has published over 7,000 stories written by children from all over the world. It also includes an online chat area where children can meet and talk and a message center to leave notes for others. Kidpub Schools gives classes the opportunity to publish their writing for children at other schools to read and comment on. You can find Kidpub at http://www.kidpub.org/kidpub/.

More and more schools, particularly in North America, are getting connected to the Internet. In Great Britain, Project Connect, a group that includes educational establishments, local and national governments, charities, and major information technology manufacturers, is aiming to connect around 30,000 schools in Great Britain to the Internet. Every school will be able to purchase low-cost Internet systems from a variety of manufacturers and will be given the opportunity to create their own Web pages.

The Internet allows students to share problems and discoveries with one another in ways that were unheard of before. Meeting in virtual classrooms through their computers, students can communicate with one another outside normal schooltime. The benefits for students unable to reach the school, because of illness, adverse weather conditions, or living in isolated communities, are huge.

The Internet has the advantage of providing up-to-date information faster than any book or magazine publisher can make it available. Students wanting to know more about the latest space mission can go straight to the NASA site and download all the information they need. Even students uncomfortable with typing on a computer keyboard can point and click their way around the Web.

Mail groups

Teachers working on similar subjects can form mail groups to share techniques, materials, and ideas. A teacher in Austria asked her students to survey the water quality in nearby small streams. Next she asked them to discover which high schools on the Internet also happened to lie at the same latitude (45 degrees) north of the equator. The students contacted these schools and sent them the survey by e-mail, asking them to test water quality in their area. The data that came back to Austria over the Internet was used by the students to give a picture of small-stream water quality along the same latitude. It is difficult to imagine how a school could complete a project like this before the Internet came along.

Like large companies, schools can have an intranet where students can share their work and have an ongoing electronic school magazine. There also can be links to the outside world, allowing parents to log on to the school web and keep up-to-date with the school's activities and even e-mail teachers with queries and suggestions. All of this could help to integrate schools into their communities, making education a shared responsibility.

The data gathered for a school project can be recorded on a computer and then sent over the Internet to students at schools all over the world.

INTO THE FUTURE

What will the Internet be like in a few years? Prediction is a risky business, especially when dealing with something that evolves as rapidly as the Internet. It is amazing to think that only two or three years ago very few people had even heard of it.

RealAudio, a program that turns your computer into a radio, makes it possible to receive sound broadcasts on the Internet. Whole concerts have been sent over the Internet. It opens up the possibility for other music events, as well as sporting events, theater, and talk shows to be broadcast live to the Internet. Download a copy of RealAudio from http://www.realaudio.com and tune in to http://www. audionet.com to find out what is happening.

The program CU-See-Me offers a video link between computers. As long as both you and the person you are connected with each have a video camera plugged into your computers, you will be able to see each other. Unfortunately because a visual image takes up a lot of data, the quality is poor if you do not have a very fast modem.

Playing a computer game. On the Internet, you can download games or consult an online encyclopedia, which includes sound and video clips.

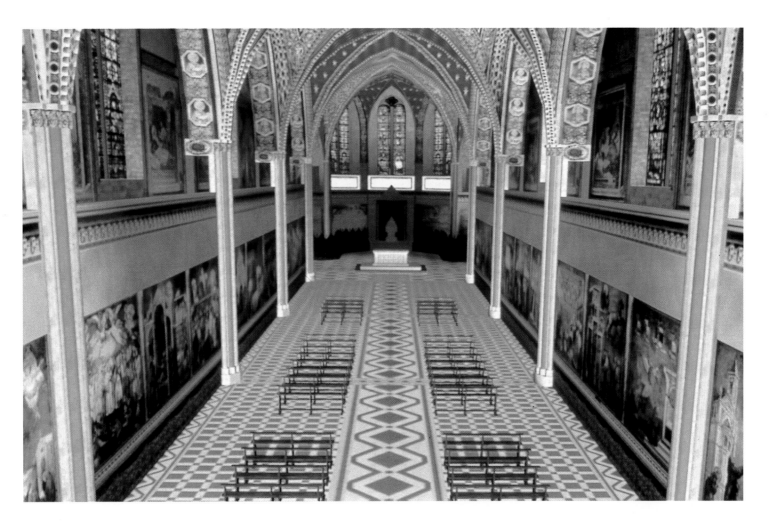

New browsers, such as WebSpace®, are offering the possibility of exploring 3-D virtual worlds. Computer-made and animated objects can be viewed from all angles. For instance, a 3-D representation of a famous museum could be downloaded to your machine, so that you could tour the exhibits without leaving your chair. This feature also demands very fast rates of data transfer and powerful computers to process the data.

Despite the limitations, it is possible to hold an online video-conference with people all over the world, or to consult an online encyclopedia complete with sound and video clips. Or you can download the latest game in exchange for a fee. Your computer can act like a cable television, enabling you to see television broadcasts from around the world. The Internet could transform the computer into the entertainment and information-gathering center of your home.

It is already possible to play some computer games with several people across the Internet. In the future you may be able to explore virtual reality buildings like this.

THE COMMUNICATIONS REVOLUTION

There can be no doubt that the way we communicate with one another is changing. We now have easy access to more information than at any time in the past. The Internet has given ordinary people the ability to get in touch with others in a way that would never have been thought possible even fifty years ago.

The Internet is set to become more personal in the future, offering people the ability to customize the way they use it, and to set up their own information-gathering sites. Firefly, at http://www.firefly.com, keeps track of your tastes in music, movies, books, and other forms of entertainment by asking questions and noting how you answer. It uses this information to keep you in touch with other things you might enjoy. It also offers chat rooms where you can discuss things with people who have similar tastes to yours. Yahoo! offers a personalized search engine called My Yahoo (http://my.yahoo.com), which will find Web sites that suit your tastes. It all helps to make surfing the Internet much less of a "hit or miss" affair.

You need to think carefully about what you see on the Internet. Along with reports on serious scientific projects, such as the one searching for evidence for life on Mars (above), you can find sites dealing with popular but unscientific subjects, such as UFO sightings (right) and crop circles (opposite top).

A final word

Perhaps here we should end with a brief word of advice. Every month more and more people sign up to the Internet, looking for information and entertainment, or simply because they want to keep up with the times. The Internet can indeed provide a great deal of entertainment and valuable information. It gives us the ability to send our ideas to thousands, perhaps millions of other people, and it gives them the chance to send their ideas to us.

So think about what you are saying before you send it. Think about what you are reading on your screen. Just because it is on a computer does not necessarily make it true. All of the personalized filters in the world cannot replace the best information filter you have—your brain.

Being cybersmart will be a big advantage in the electronic world that is growing rapidly around us.

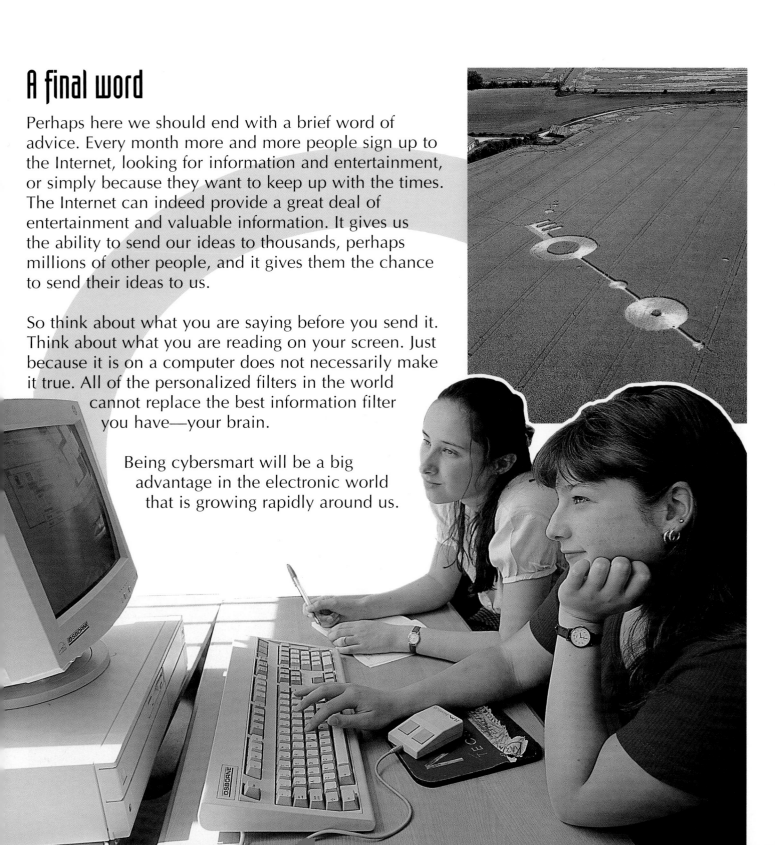

DATE CHART

1957 The Soviet Union launches Sputnik, the first artificial satellite, and the U.S. Department of Defense sets up the Advanced Research Projects Agency (ARPA) to get the United States back in front in the arms race.

1969 ARPANET is commissioned by the U.S. Department of Defense for research into computer networking. The first nodes are set up at UCLA, the Stanford Research Institute, UCSB, and the University of Utah.

1970 ARPANET hosts start using the Network Control Protocol (NCP).

1971 The ARPANET increases to fifteen nodes, which includes NASA.

1972 The International Conference on Computer Communications is shown a demonstration of ARPANET, involving thirty-seven machines. An e-mail program is invented to send messages across a network.

1973 The first international ARPANET connections to Great Britain and Norway are established.

1982 The Transmission Control Protocol (TCP) and Internet Protocol (IP) are established for ARPANET. An "internet" is defined as a connected set of networks using TCP/IP and the "Internet" as a number of connected TCP/IP internets.

1983 ARPANET splits into ARPANET and MILNET, the military net.

1984 The number of hosts exceeds 1,000.

1986 NSFNET is created with five super-computing centers offering high-speed computing power. The number of connections from universities increases dramatically.

1987 The number of hosts exceeds 10,000.

1989 The number of hosts exceeds 100,000.

1990 ARPANET ceases to exist.

1991 The World Wide Web, developed by Tim Berners-Lee, is released by CERN. The number of hosts exceeds 1,000,000.

1993 The White House goes online for the first time, as do the United Nations and World Bank. Mosaic, the first graphical Web browser, brings about a staggering 341,634 percent increase in Web traffic.

1994 Online shopping arrives.

1995 RealAudio offers Net users the ability to hear live audio broadcasts through their computers.

1996 The estimated number of Net users exceeds 35 million.

PICK A PLACE TO GO

Many Web sites change their addresses over time. If you do not find something at the address listed, try using a search engine to locate it.

AltaVista
http://www.altavista.digital.
com
A search engine.

CityNet
http://www.city.net
Gives information on the world's major cities.

CNN
http://www.cnn.com
The web site of the Cable News Network (CNN).

The Electronic Zoo
http://netvet.wustl.edu/
e-zoo.htm
Information on the living world.

Global SchoolNet Foundation
http://www.gsn.org
Links children around the world.

Happy Puppy
http://www.happypuppy.com
A huge site dedicated to computer games.

Internet Public Library
http://www.ipl.org
A huge resource of information.

Just for Kids
http://www.aone.com/
~mrbill/kids.html
Many links to great pages for children across the Internet. Written by children for children.

KidsCom
http://www.kidscom.com
A place where children can meet other children online, and a place where their parents can meet.

New Scientist
http://www.newscientist.com
A first-class site for up-to-date science news and information.

Space Calendar
http://newproducts.jpl.nasa.
gov/calendar/
Keeps track of the latest astronomical events.

Yahooligans!
http://www.yahooligans.com
A search engine for children.

GLOSSARY

access To make use of information stored in a computer.

address Every computer linked to the Internet has a unique address that locates it on the Internet. A World Wide Web site has an address called a Uniform Resource Locator (URL). Individual Internet users have e-mail addresses.

arms race The period after World War II when the United States and the Soviet Union tried to outdo each other in terms of the weapons they produced.

bit (Binary DigIT) The smallest unit of computer data, a single binary number, either a 1 or a zero. Bandwidth and modem speed is usually measured in bits per second (bps).

cable television A system for sending many different television channels by cable to people who pay for the service.

credit card A card issued by a bank or a business that allows someone to buy goods and pay for them later.

data Information in a form suitable for use by a computer.

databases Collections of data arranged for easy retrieval of the information they contain.

dish antenna A device for sending and receiving communication signals.

download To transfer data or programs from a central server computer to another computer.

files Data records held on a computer.

graphic Data displayed by a computer in the form of a picture.

host Any computer on a network that allows users to communicate with other computers on the network. If you use a service provider to get on to the Internet, their computer is acting as your host.

icon A symbol displayed on the computer screen.

leased-line A phone line that provides a permanent connection between one location and another. The highest-speed connections require a leased line.

laptop computer A computer with a built-in screen and keyboard, small enough to be easily transported and used almost anywhere.

logging on Entering into a computer system. For example, you log on when you dial your service provider.

mailing list A system that allows people to send e-mail to a single address where it is copied and sent on to all of the other subscribers to the mailing list. This allows people to participate in discussions with others.

microwave relay stations Stations that transmit radio broadcasts and phone signals in the form of microwaves. Microwaves are part of the whole range of waves called the electromagnetic spectrum (EMS). This includes ordinary light rays (rays that we can see), infrared rays, and ultraviolet rays.

mouse A device for moving an indicator around on a computer screen and for activating programs.

netiquette The etiquette, or the way you should behave, on the Internet.

node Any computer connected to a network.

offline Not connected to a computer network.

online Connected to a computer network.

program A set of coded information that instructs a computer to perform a particular task.

router A computer that handles the connection between one network and another. Routers direct packets of information through the networks to their destinations.

satellite ground station A place where signals are beamed up to, and received from, satellites orbiting far above the Earth.

server Software on a computer that provides a service to client software on computers elsewhere. For example, a mail server would handle e-mail for various client machines.

software The set of programs that control the operations performed by a computer (the hardware).

subscribers People who pay for a service such as cable television or an Internet connection.

supercomputers Large computers, often serving several terminals, that are among the fastest and most powerful computers available.

telephone exchange A building where telephone lines are connected.

video conference A meeting carried out using video cameras so that people in different offices can both see and speak to each other as if they were in the same room.

virtual (worlds) Computer simulations of real or imaginary objects or places that can be explored by the computer user.

FIND OUT MORE

Books to read

Borman, Jami Lynn. *A Computer Dictionary for Kids...And Their Parents*. Hauppauge, NY: Barron's Educational Series, Inc., 1995.

Brimner, Larry D. *World Wide Web*. Danbury, CT: Children's Press, 1997.

Cochrane, Kerry. *Internet*. First Books. Danbury, CT: Franklin Watts, 1995.

Pederson, Ted & Moss, Francis. *Internet for Kids: A Beginner's Guide to Surfing the Net*. Los Angeles: Price Stern Sloan, 1995.

Polly, Jean. *Internet Kid's Yellow Pages*. New York: McGraw Hill, 1996.

INDEX